Learn About

YOUR BE...

I Can Be Kind

written by Meredith Rusu

illustrated by Alexandra Colombo

Children's Press®
An imprint of Scholastic Inc.

Special thanks to Doctor Ann (Nancy) Close, Assistant Professor of the
Yale School of Medicine and member of the Child Study Center at Yale University,
for her insight into the development of children in early childhood.

Thank you also to Swati Parikh for consulting on the appropriate
dress for our protagonist and her family.

Library of Congress Cataloging-in-Publication Data available
ISBN 978-1-339-02057-0 (library binding) | ISBN 978-1-339-02058-7 (paperback)

10 9 8 7 6 5 4 3 2 1   24 25 26 27 28

Printed in China, 62
First edition, 2024

Book design by Kathleen Petelinsek

TABLE OF CONTENTS

I Can Be Kind

Hello! I am Allina. Do you like to be kind? I do! It makes people feel good and happy. It makes me feel good and happy, too!

But did you know **KINDNESS SPREADS**? Here are some ways I choose to be kind every day.

Watch what happens!

I can be kind by saying "Good morning!" to Mommy and Daddy.

I like to give them a big "good morning" hug, too.

KINDNESS SPREADS!
Mommy laughs when I squeeze her tight.

I can be kind by saying "thank you" for breakfast.

Even if Daddy makes me eggs instead of my favorite breakfast, pancakes.

The eggs are just the way I like them— and I tell him they're yummy!

KINDNESS SPREADS!

Daddy helps me clean up my spilled milk. He knows it was an accident.

I can be kind by picking up my friend's glove when he drops it going into school.

I don't want his hand to be cold at recess later.

KINDNESS SPREADS!

My friend helps me find my water bottle in the lost and found.

I can be kind by **volunteering** to pass out markers in class.

It takes less time when my teacher and I work together.

KINDNESS SPREADS!
My teacher thanks me and tells me I'm a super helper!

I can be kind by cheering my friends on in gym class.

Even if they don't make a goal, they gave it their best shot.

KINDNESS SPREADS!

My friend asks if I want to kick the ball back and forth.

15

I can be kind by asking someone who is alone if they'd like to sit with me at lunch.

It's more fun eating together.

KINDNESS SPREADS!

My new friend shows me his trading cards!

SHOW-AND-
TELL

Aa Bb Cc
Dd Ee Ff
Gg Hh Ii
Jj Kk

60+10

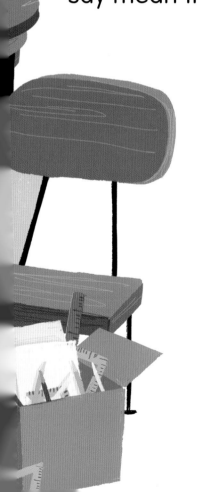

I can be kind by telling someone that I like what they brought to show-and-tell.

Some of the other kids think it looks weird.

But our teacher reminds us it's not kind to say mean things.

KINDNESS SPREADS!

My friend tells me she likes the decorations on my backpack!

I can be kind by asking a friend to help me move ladybugs off the playground. I don't want them to get squished!

They're so tiny—they need our help to reach a warm, safe place.

KINDNESS SPREADS!

Now everyone wants to help the ladybugs, too!

I can be kind by saying "Oh no! Are you okay?" when I step on my friend's foot.

I was being too silly. I should have been paying better attention.

KINDNESS SPREADS!

My friend says it's all right. She knows I didn't mean to.

See? When I choose kindness, it spreads everywhere.

That makes everyone feel happy!

I also feel calm inside. I feel stronger.

And that is an amazing **feeling**!

A a

E e

I i

AFTERCARE
3PM - 5PM

B b C c D d
F f G g H h
J j   L l

CHOOSING KINDNESS

Every day, our brain makes our body do things on its own to stay alive and healthy. For example, breathing and keeping our heart beating.

But our brain can't make us be kind by itself. Kindness is a *choice*. That means we decide if we want to be kind or not. When we choose kindness, our lives are much happier.

Read the sentences on the opposite page with an adult. Which children are choosing kindness? Which ones aren't? How would you change their **behavior** to be more kind?

A boy picks up litter from the ground and throws it in the trash can.

A girl pushes her friend on the swing.

A boy fills a birdfeeder with fresh birdseed for the blue jays.

An older brother grabs the video game controller from his younger sister so he can play what he wants.

A boy says "You're weird!" to another kid on the playground.

A student gives her teacher a handmade "thank you" card.

Now think of a time when you were kind to someone. How did it make you feel? How do you think the other person felt?

LET'S BE KIND!

Kindness can feel good in lots of different ways! Sometimes being kind makes you feel calm inside. Other times it makes you feel stronger. You might even feel like you're smiling all over when you're kind because you are so proud of yourself!

Try these simple ways to be kind—and watch what happens!

Give five friends a high five during the day. (Give them a compliment, too.)

Ask your parents what they did while you were at school.

Write your grandparents or other family member a letter or draw them a picture. Have your parents help you put it in an envelope and mail it to them.

When you want to play a game, ask your friend what game they would like to play first.

Teach a friend how to do something you're good at, like drawing a cartoon or jumping rope.

Once you did these, did you notice that kindness spreads?

GLOSSARY

behavior (bi-HAYV-yur) the way someone acts
My friend's silly behavior made me laugh.

choice (CHOIS) the chance to choose something or not
I have the choice of playing basketball or soccer this summer.

compliment (KAHM-pluh-muhnt) a remark or action that shows you appreciate something
The lady complimented my pretty shoes.

feeling (FEE-ling) a thought or emotion
I had a happy feeling when my favorite show came on television.

kindness (KINDE-nis) being friendly, helpful, and generous

Sharing her cookie was an act of kindness.

spreads (SPREDZ) distributes or makes something more widely shared

Excitement spread throughout the students when they heard tomorrow would be a snow day.

volunteering (vah-luhn-TEER-ing) freely offering to do something

She loved volunteering at the animal shelter and feeding the bunnies.

ABOUT THE AUTHOR

Meredith Rusu has written more than 100 children's books. She lives in New Jersey with her husband and two young sons whom she tries (very hard!) to remind to be kind every day.

ABOUT THE ILLUSTRATOR

Alexandra Colombo has illustrated more than 100 books that have been published all over the world. She loves walking in the woods, writing poetry, and discovering new places. She lives in Italy with her dog, Ary, and her turtle, Carlo.